Allen Jay and the UNDERGROUND RAILROAD

by Marlene Targ Brill
illustrated by Janice Lee Porter

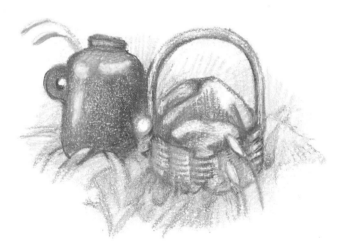

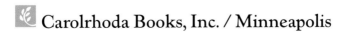
Carolrhoda Books, Inc. / Minneapolis

For Alison and her grandmother, Genevieve, two people who enjoy action-packed stories and a little history—MTB

To Jai—JLP

Note to readers: Many members of the Society of Friends during the 1880s said "thee" for "you" in most all situations, rather than using both thee and thou.

Special thanks to the many generous people who helped gather and verify information for this book, especially Sabron R. Newton, librarian for the 57th Street Friends Meeting, Chicago; Thomas Hamm, archivist at Erlham University; Kamau Sababu Kambui, a historian and naturalist who specializes in the history of the Underground Railroad; Gerald Canter, professor emeritus at the Department of Communications Sciences and Disorders, Northwestern University; the staff of the Wilmette Public Library (Illinois); and Marybeth Lorbiecki, editor.

This book is available in two editions:
Library binding by Carolrhoda Books, Inc., a division of Lerner Publishing Group
Soft cover by First Avenue Editions, an imprint of Lerner Publishing Group
241 First Avenue North
Minneapolis, MN 55401 U.S.A.

Website address: www.lernerbooks.com

Library of Congress Cataloging-in-Publication Data

Brill, Marlene Targ.
    Allen Jay and the Underground Railroad / by Marlene Targ Brill ; illustrated by Janice Lee Porter.
        p.   cm.
    Summary: Recounts how Allen Jay, a young Quaker boy living in Ohio during the 1840s, helped a fleeing slave escape his master and make it to freedom through the Underground Railroad.
    ISBN 0-87614-776-7 (lib. bdg. : alk. paper)
    ISBN 0-87614-605-1 (pbk. : alk. paper)
    1. Underground Railroad – Juvenile literature. 2. Fugitive slaves – United States – Juvenile literature. 3. Jay, Allen – Juvenile literature. 4. Slavery and the church – Society of Friends – Juvenile literature. 5. Quakers – United States – History – 19th century – Juvenile literature. [1. Underground railroad. 2. Fugitive slaves. 3. Jay, Allen. 4. Quakers.]
    I. Porter, Janice Lee, ill. II. Title.
E450.T17 1993
973.7'115 – dc20   92-25279

Manufactured in the United States of America
11 12 13 14 15 16 – DP – 09 08 07 06 05 04

Author's Note

Allen Jay and his family lived in Randolph, Ohio, during the 1840s. The Jays belonged to a religious group called the Society of Friends, or Quakers. Friends believed everyone was equal. So they dressed alike in plain clothes and called everybody "thee," whether stranger or friend. Sadly, most African Americans who lived in the Southern United States were not treated as equals. They were slaves. Slaves worked all day without pay. Their bosses claimed to own them like animals. Any slaves who escaped were hunted and punished. They were often tortured or killed. People who helped slaves escape were punished too.

Allen's parents, Isaac and Rhoda Jay, helped slaves run away even though it was dangerous. The Jays were part of a secret group called the Underground Railroad.

People who worked with the Underground Railroad hid runaway slaves in their barns, attics, and hidden rooms. They guided the runaways from one safe place to the next. Runaways traveled by foot, wagon, or horseback, following secret routes to Canada. There, everyone was treated equally under the law.

The Jays were careful not to tell others what they did—not even their children. Eleven-year-old Allen knew that his parents fed and hid dark strangers who appeared and disappeared mysteriously. But he didn't understand much about slavery—until the day he came face-to-face with a runaway.

July 1, 1842

Allen hung
the last shirt on the line.
His mother was too sick
to do such heavy work.
So the job fell to her eldest child.
Every Monday Allen washed, boiled,
starched, and hung out the clothes.
Afterward he was free to play.

5

This afternoon
Allen headed for the barn
to get his fishing pole.
As he crossed the front yard,
he saw a horse racing down the road
toward the Jay farm.
Within seconds
the family doctor stopped
at the front gate.

"Friend Jay! Friend Jay!"
the doctor shouted.
Allen's father came out of the barn
and walked quickly to the gate.
"Thy horse has wings today,"
said Isaac Jay.
"Thee seems in a hurry."

The doctor leaned toward Isaac.
"A runaway slave is hiding
in the woods," the doctor said
in a low voice.

"The slave's owner and his men
are following close behind,
and they have guns," he warned.
The doctor grabbed Isaac's shoulder
and added, "Be careful, my friend."
Allen's father nodded.
The doctor turned his horse
and rode away.
Allen moved closer to his father
and looked up into his troubled face.
Allen wondered,
Would the slave's owner come
and shoot his father?
He remembered stories
about other Friends
who helped runaways.
Some Friends had been beaten.
Others had had their homes burned.

Isaac Jay looked down at his son.
"Allen," his father said,
"thee may soon see
a dark-skinned man.
Take him into the cornfield
behind the big walnut tree.
The corn is high enough there
to hide him.
But if thee does this,
thee must not tell me or anyone."
Then Isaac Jay turned
and walked back to the barn.

Allen could not move.
What should he do now?
A crackling sound from the woods
broke into Allen's thoughts.
He saw someone moving
through the trees and brush.
Allen walked quietly
toward the sounds.
The rustling stopped.

Suddenly a man with a gun
leaped out of the brush.
Allen jumped back.
The two of them stared at each other
without speaking.
The man had ragged clothes
and bloody feet.
His dark skin was cut
and scarred with whip burns.
"Is you Marster Jay's boy?"
the man demanded.
His eyes darted back and forth,
watching the road and the house.
"Yes," Allen stammered,
"I'm Allen, his son."
The man lowered his gun.

Allen gathered his courage to speak.
He had always had trouble
saying words clearly.
Now it was more important
than ever to be understood.
"Follow me," Allen said slowly.
"Father told me to take you
to a hiding place."
"I understand," the man said.

Allen led him along the edge of the
woods to the back of the farm.
They bent over
as they ran deep into the cornfield.
Allen brought the man to a clearing
under the walnut tree.
"Thee must stay quiet and out of sight,"
Allen whispered.
"Someone will come for thee in time."

"Have mercy," the man begged.
"My name is Henry James.
I ran away day before last,
and I ain't had nothing to eat
or drink since."
His eyes looked sad and tired.
His lips were cracked
from the heat.

"I will come back soon with some food,"
Allen told him.
The boy looked around to make
sure no one could see Henry James.
He broke off a cornstalk
and stirred the dirt behind him
as he walked to cover any footprints.
He checked that
all the cornstalks were in place.
Then Allen ran through
the woods to the house.
He hoped the slave owner
was hours away.
His father would need time to plan
a safe escape for this runaway.
Allen slowed his footsteps
as he neared the barn.
Someone might be watching,
he thought.

Allen opened the kitchen door.
Milton, Walter, Abijah, and Mary
were shelling peas at the table.
His mother got up
from her rocking chair.
"Sit down, Allen," she ordered
in a quiet voice.
"I have something for thee."
"But, Mother," Allen protested.
"Hush, son," she said.
Allen slid onto the bench next to Walter.
"Mary, please put some corn bread
and bacon into a basket,"
Rhoda Jay said.
Allen wondered how his mother
knew to fix food at this odd hour
of the day.
And why were his brothers
and sister all inside?

"Who gets the corn bread?"
asked little Milton.
"Any friend who may pass our way,"
answered his mother, smiling.

Rhoda Jay handed
the filled basket to Allen.
"Take this basket to anybody
thee thinks is hungry," she said.
Allen took the basket
and grabbed a jug of milk.
Then he hurried back
to the cornfield.

As he got near the walnut tree,
Allen heard stalks snapping.
A dark gun barrel poked
through the corn.
Allen froze.
Click!
He knew the gun was ready to fire.

"Please, don't shoot," begged the boy.

Henry lowered the gun
and pushed the corn aside.

"You give me a scare,"
Henry said, his voice shaking.

Allen let out a deep sigh
and moved closer.

"Help thyself," Allen said,
showing the man what he brought.

Henry grabbed the jug.

He took a long, hearty drink.

"This be mighty fine, Marster Allen,"
Henry James said thankfully.

"Thee may rest here
until my father comes for thee.
I must go now," Allen said.

Allen pushed through the corn
to the edge of the field.
He heard voices
as he came through the woods.
He ducked behind a pile of firewood
before anyone saw him.
Allen peeked through the logs
and saw his father facing
six men on horseback.
The strangers had guns.

A man questioned his father roughly,
"Are you sure you didn't
see my runaway?"
Isaac Jay shook his head.
"I told thee once.
I never speak falsehoods."
The slave owner snorted
in disbelief.
"Then how about a look
through your house?" he yelled.
"Thee are welcome,"
said Isaac Jay quietly.
"But thee needs the correct papers."
"That could take some time,"
the owner shouted.
"Expect us back by morning."
Then he grumbled to his men,
and they rode off in a hurry.

Allen heard nothing more
about the runaway slave
or the angry men that afternoon.
And he dared not ask.
When Isaac Jay came inside for supper,
he said little.
That night Allen's mother
sent the younger children to bed early.
Allen's father went out to the barn.
A little while later,
he came to the door
and called Allen outside.
Old Jack, their horse, stood in the yard
harnessed to the buggy.
"How would thee like to go
to thy grandfather's house?"
Isaac Jay said to his son.
"Go along with thee?"
Allen asked, puzzled.

"No, by thyself this time,"
his father answered.
Allen had never traveled through
the woods in the dark before.
There were bears, wildcats,
and snakes out there.
Now there might be slave hunters too.
But Allen knew what his father
wanted him to do.

Allen's mother came outside
and clutched her husband's arm.
"Thee must not send *him*," she said,
"it's too dangerous."
"But I have to go, Mother," Allen said,
"If the owner and his men
come back tonight, Father must be here."

"I'm proud of thee, son," Isaac Jay said.
"If thee knows of anybody
who ought to go along,
thee had better take him too."

Rhoda Jay gave her son a long hug.

Allen climbed into the buggy
and grabbed the reins.

"Go quickly, and stay on the main road,"
his father cautioned.

"Thee can spend the night
at thy grandfather's house."

Allen guided Old Jack to the cornfield.

He stopped the buggy on the side of
the field near the walnut tree.

"It's Allen," he called softly.

"We must hurry."

Henry James pulled himself into the buggy
and squeezed into the space by Allen's feet.

They rode past the warm light shining
from the farmhouse windows.
A cloud passed in front of the moon.
Darkness closed around them
on the bumpy road.
Neither Allen nor Henry
said a word.
Would the slave hunters
try to catch them?
Allen tried not to think
about how scared he was.
What if Henry shot him
so he could steal Old Jack?
Allen tugged at the reins
to make Old Jack go faster.
His hands felt wet.
He bit his lower lip.

"Is you afraid to be with me?"
Henry asked.
Allen could not answer.
"Here, Marster Allen,
you carry the gun," Henry said.
"If you see anybody coming,
give it back quick.
I'll jump out as you drive.
I don't want you hurt."
He handed the gun up to Allen.
The boy shook his head.
He could not touch the gun.
"I ain't never goin' to go back,"
Henry vowed.
"They all can kill me,
but I had my last whippin'."

Then Henry told Allen stories
about being a slave.
Henry had worked all day and
most nights in the fields of Kentucky.
He had seen his brother
beaten to death.

His sister had been sold
to another owner far away.
Now Henry was determined
to reach freedom in Canada.
Allen felt bad that
he had not trusted Henry.

All at once, Allen heard something
thrashing through the leaves.
His body started to shake.
A shadow darted in front of the buggy.

Old Jack reared up on his back legs.
Allen pulled back on the reins
until his fingers ached.
Slowly the horse calmed down.

"What happened?" whispered Henry.
"Do you need the gun?"
"No," said Allen with a nervous giggle.
"It was just an old rabbit
crossing the road."
Henry didn't laugh.

Allen and Henry rode for more
than an hour and a half.
Allen worried that every shadow
was a slave hunter.
He was growing sleepy.
His back ached.
He was cold from the damp night.
And he was tired of being afraid.

Finally Allen saw a light.
It was coming from a cabin—
Grandfather Jay's cabin.

Allen jumped from the buggy
and helped Henry out.
Allen pounded on the door.
His grandfather greeted them
in his nightclothes.
Grandfather Jay seemed surprised,
but he knew what to do.
"Hurry inside, you two,"
said the elder Jay.
"Allen, wake thy uncle Levi."

Allen did as he was told.
Uncle Levi dressed
and left to saddle the horses.
Grandfather bundled some food
into a cloth sack for Henry.
Henry thanked Grandfather Jay
and followed him into the barnyard.

Before Henry and Levi rode away,
Allen held out his hand to Henry.
"May thee have a safe trip to Canada,"
Allen said, as carefully as he could.
His words sounded strong and clear.
Henry James took the boy's hand.
"I be remembering you, Marster Jay,"
he said, shaking Allen's hand.
"You is a brave boy."

Afterword

Thirty minutes later, Henry and Levi entered a large camp of free African Americans in Mercer County, Ohio. The settlement was an important stop along the Underground Railroad. A family in the camp hid Henry until it was safe to head north. Within a few months, the Jays heard that Henry had reached Canada.

Allen grew up to become a well-known Quaker minister and teacher. He was also a famous speaker, and this amazed many people. Allen was born with a hole in the roof of his mouth that made him hard to understand sometimes. But his powerful words of peace and love were treasured by many Friends. As an older man, Allen wrote the story of his life and his meeting with the runaway slave in *The Autobiography of Allen Jay.*

The Underground Railroad stayed in business until after the Civil War. This war between the states brought an end to slavery in America. By then, more than 60,000 runaway slaves had passed to freedom through the railroad. The number was small compared to the four million people who had been slaves. But the Underground Railroad's success struck a severe blow to those who wanted slavery. Young Allen Jay and other railroad conductors helped end one of the cruelest practices in the history of the United States.